Dearest Kitty

ANNE FRANK: THEN AND NOW

REV. KENNETH W EKDAHL

ISBN: 979-8-89031-871-8 (sc)
ISBN: 979-8-89031-872-5 (hc)
ISBN: 979-8-89031-873-2 (e)

One Galleria Blvd., Suite 1900, Metairie, LA 70001
(504) 702-6708

PROLOGUE

The beginning of this work actually began almost two years ago, but events that occurred last October, this past Spring, the last several weeks, and finally, this last week reinvigorated my spirit to continue with my story. October 2, 2020, I wrote Timothy Cardinal Dolan, the Archbishop of New York, stating that I was writing him for two reasons: first, to seek his help in pursuing the process of beatification and canonization for Anne Frank, her sister, Margot, and their mother, Edith, along with the millions of people who suffered and died in the Holocaust; and second, to make Anne Frank's story-initially revealed through *The Diary of a Young Girl,* published in late July of 1947-more well-known, certainly to young people, but to all ages. Cardinal Dolan wrote me immediately and very graciously thanked me, but also stated very clearly that beatification and canonization is reserved for practicing Catholics! But he also assured me that my goal to make Anne Frank's story better known was a worthy one.

The actual date prompting this story occurred on April 17, 1968, when my classmate, Mike Burke, and I met Otto Frank in a downstairs diner across the street from the annex where Otto Frank, his wife, Edith, and their two daughters, Margot and Anne, hid from the Nazis, along with five others, for over two years until they were probably betrayed and captured. In the end, Edith Frank probably succumbed in the Bergen-Belsen concentration camp in January of 1945; Margot probably passed in late March, and Anne died perhaps a few days later in early April of 1945. The others also died in concentration camps. Only Otto Frank survived and was released perhaps days before the Russian army freed those who remained at Bergen-Belsen just as World War II was nearing its end.

As I now complete this story, nearly fifty-four years have passed, and I have wanted to tell this story for a long time. As our country struggles to move beyond the COVID-19 pandemic and the events this past August when thirteen Americans were murdered in Afghanistan- well, it is difficult to comprehend. Perhaps it's the horrific conditions maintained at our southern border and the absolute abandonment of securing our country's borders, but I sincerely believe Anne Frank's story needs to be read again. I believe it is my calling to reawaken people to her story as first told in *The Diary of a Young Girl.* I confirm my belief that the Lord was indeed with the millions who suffered and died-Jews, Christians, Moslems-everyone who suffered in the Holocaust of the Second World War, who are now with God for all eternity. I am indebted to Cardinal Dolan for correcting me, but I will also make it clear why I believe Anne Frank is in Heaven.

CHAPTER 1

Then[MC3]

On September 5, 1961, I entered Christian Brothers Academy (CBA) in Lincroft, N.J., an all-boys school, as a first-year. Although it wouldn't dawn on me for many years, that first week would establish my future courses of study as I selected two language courses: Introduction to Latin 1 and Spanish 1. These decisions would influence future ones made some seven years later. After graduating from CBA in 1965, I travelled with six underclassmen to Rio Piedras, Puerto Rico, primarily to teach religion but also to teach mathematics, geography, art, etc. to los ninos de los barrios[MC4]. Fortunately, we had the help of several Cuban high school girls who spoke both languages. Three years of Spanish at CBA helped me when I entered Mount St. Mary's College (now University) in Emmitsburg, MD, an-all male school at the time. During my sophomore year at the Mount, five students, including myself, applied to Loyola of Rome University, along with one young woman from St. Joseph's College, also in Emmitsburg. We were all accepted.

The junior year class (67/68) of Loyola University of Rome accepted some 250 students, consisting of roughly half-male and half-female.

Travel was encouraged for both near and far[MC5]. There was but one stipulation: each student must maintain a B- average to travel outside the city of Rome.

Arriving at Loyola during the first week of September 1967, the students began to experience the Loyola campus, with all the historical, cultural, and religious opportunities that were awaiting them. The Roman campus of Loyola offered generous time away from class with every other Friday off, along with ten days for Thanksgiving and three weeks for both Christmas and Easter. Indeed, Loyola did provide these benefits but only if one maintained the minimum requirements. Sadly, there were a few who rarely left the campus.

For Thanksgiving, I traveled with three classmates by car to visit Greece and Turkey, returning though the communist countries of Bulgaria and Yugoslavia, staying at an army base the first night. I remember I was scared to death because we snuck onto the base. The second night we stayed in Trieste in northern Italy. The pensione was on the sixth floor (no elevator) and the temperature in this large room was probably in the high thirties. For Christmas vacation I traveled by train to Madrid, Spain, and somehow read the entire *Don Quixote* novel in Spanish for the duration of the trip. Lastly, I traveled by air with my classmate Michael Burke, first visiting Amsterdam, Holland, followed by flights to Paris, France, London, England and then to our last stop in Lake Zurich, Switzerland before returning to Rome to complete the remaining classes at Loyola.

Our first morning in Amsterdam on April 15, 1968, Mike and I took the trolley out to the Heineken Brewery to take in a forty minute tour followed by a sampling of their product for several hours. Although our initial plan would've included a stop at the Raikes Museum that afternoon, we returned to our pensione for sorely needed nap time. The following day we toured the aforementioned Raikes Museum for most of the day. On the morning of April 17, 1968, Mike and I visited the annex, the Anne Frank Fonds (Foundation) where Otto and Edith Frank and their daughters, Margot and Anne, hid away from the Nazis, along with five other individuals for over two years.

We all live with the objective of being happy;
our lives are all different and yet the same.[MC6]- 4

CHAPTER 2

Then and Now

Having read *The Diary of Anne Frank* during my first-year at Christian Brothers Academy (CBA) in Lincroft, N.J., the tour of the hiding place in the annex[MC8] awakened me to a profound understanding of the Diary I had first read at CBA.

Completing the tour, we exited into the gift shop where I immediately purchased a new copy of *The Diary of a Young Girl* with fresh knowledge as to where they had hidden out, which, sadly, was in vain. Mike Burke and I crossed the street diagonally and entered a diner below street level and were seated at a small booth. As we ordered lunch, an elderly gentleman appeared and asked if he might sit with us for lunch. Mike moved in and invited him to sit. He seemed to know his way around the menu, quickly making his selection.

This gentleman asked if he could see one of my books, and I promptly handed him the popular *Europe on Five Dollars a Day* book. However, shaking his head, I offered him the other book, *The Diary of a Young Girl.* For the next twenty-five minutes or so, Otto Frank spoke of the Anne Frank Fonds (Foundation). He described its purpose and how it serves to bring its message to all who visit the premises. This man seemed eager to preserve the story of Anne Frank and to describe the courage this young girl possessed. He insisted on how its story must be told and remembered. It would be many years later that I would be struck by the similarity of Otto Frank's story to that of the Emmaus story in Luke's Gospel (Luke 24: 13-35). Two disciples of Jesus would encounter a man who told them of the Hebrew Scriptures that we have come to identify with the Old Testament. After Jesus disappeared from their sight, the disciples said to each other, "Were not our hearts burning (within us) while He spoke to us on the way and opened the Scriptures to us?"

This gentleman with whom Mike and I had lunch that day picked up our lunch receipts, handed me his business card, paid for our lunch, climbed the steps, and disappeared from view. As our lunch friend left, I opened his card and glanced at his name: Otto H. Frank. I vividly recall how my heart was burning as it really dawned on me with whom we had just eaten lunch-Otto Frank! Anne Frank's father! I remember reflecting on how so much of life's joys are frequently bittersweet and how much this gentle man must have suffered with the loss of his wife, Edith, and his two daughters, Margot and Anne, all having died in the Bergen-Belsen concentration camp.

When Mike and I met Otto Frank on April 17, 1968, in that Amsterdam diner, Otto Frank was fast approaching his seventy-ninth birthday on May 12. He would eventually die on August 19, 1980, at the age of ninety-one. *The Diary of a Young Girl* was first published in June of 1947, some four months prior to my own birth. Over the last fifty-four years, I have made countless moves, and somewhere, somehow, the business card that Otto Frank gave me has been lost through time. While the loss of his card is regrettable, the memory of the encounter in that small Amsterdam diner is unforgettable and will forever remain deep within the depths of my heart.

CHAPTER 3

Then and Now

In the *Catechism of the Catholic Church*, Heaven and Earth, the Apostles' Creed, [MC9] professes that God is "Creator of heaven and earth." [MC10] The Nicene Creed makes it explicit that this profession includes "all that is, seen and unseen" ([i]). [MC11] The scriptural expression of "heaven and earth" means *all that exists*, creation in its entirety. It also indicates the bond, deep within creation, that unites both heaven and earth and distinguishes one from the other: "the earth" is the world of men, while "Heaven" or "the heavens" can designate both the firmament and God's own "place"-our Father in "heaven" and consequently, the "heaven" which is eschatological glory. Finally, "Heaven" refers to the saints and the "place" of the spiritual creatures, the angels who surround God ([ii]). The profession of faith of the Fourth Lateran Council (1215 A.C.E.) affirms that God "from the beginning of time made at once (simul) out of nothing both orders of creatures, the spiritual and corporeal, that is, the angelic and the earthly, and then (deinde) the human creature, who as it were shares in both orders, being composed of spirit and body" (30).

I wrote[MC12] Timothy Michael Cardinal Dolan, the Archbishop of New York, on October 2, 2020, and received a prompt letter from Cardinal Dolan on October 9, 2020. The aforementioned letter described my two-fold purpose of creating a document that would seek to make Anne Frank's diary more well known, especially to the younger people of our world, and to pursue the possibility of having Anne Frank and the millions of others who died during the Holocaust be beatified and canonized by the Roman Catholic Church. I am most appreciative of Cardinal Dolan's correcting me on my second purpose described above. I offer a frequently told story using humor to emphasize my overall purpose, which I've amended, to say that Anne Frank, her sister, Margot, her mother, Edith, and the millions of others who suffered and died in the Holocaust, should now be in Heaven.

Consider this: three people die and go to Heaven. St. Peter meets them at the pearly gates. He says to the first man, "Welcome to heaven! Back on Earth, what denomination were you?"

The first man says, "I was a devout Presbyterian."

St. Peter says, "Excellent! Then proceed to door number ten, but when you pass door number three, be very quiet!" St. Peter then asked the second person, "What denomination were you?"

She replied that she was the pastor of the Evangelical Church in London, England, St. Peter says, "Wonderful! Make your way to door number six, but when you pass door number three, be very quiet." Finally, St. Peter asks the last man standing, "What denomination were you on earth?"

The man answers, "I was a Lutheran and part of the Missouri Synod."

"Well, you know the drill. Go to door number seven, but be very quiet when you pass door number three."

This last person worked up the gumption to ask St. Peter, "Why is it that we need to be quiet when we go past door number three?"

St. Peter smiles and replies, "Because that's where the Catholics are, and they think they're the only ones up here."

Originally, when I wrote Timothy Michael Cardinal Dolan on October 2, 2020, Cardinal Dolan corrected the first of the two reasons I had written as my primary purpose for writing this book. I am most grateful for the good Cardinal's clarification, but my work continues in my belief that Edith Frank, Margot Frank, Anne Frank, and the millions of others who died during the Holocaust are indeed in Heaven.

I should lend credence to this by stating that second only to the Bible itself, *The Diary of Anne Frank* is the most widely read non-fiction book in the entire world. Of course, by itself, it *is* history. Everyone should know who Anne Frank is, and for me, her story truthfully represents the millions who perished unjustly during the Second World War. Certainly, there are many messages for me, but the most important message is that all people have the right to live in freedom. Anne Frank's diary shows us that people may practice a different religion or be of a different race or nationality, but they should never be treated any differently, more less be executed.

The Diary of Anne Frank ends on August 1, 1944, when the Nazis entered the annex and took all nine who were hiding out to their ultimate deaths, except for Otto Frank. She was youthful, optimistic with jolts of anger, irony, and humor. Her writing shows mature insights into life, war, and interpersonal relationships, notwithstanding that she would never reach the age of sixteen.

CHAPTER 4

In *The Roman Missal, Friday of the Passion of the Lord,* and the following day (Good Friday) by a most ancient tradition, the church does not celebrate the sacraments at all, except for Penance and the Anointing of the Sick. On the Friday of the Passion of the Lord, the celebration consists of three parts, namely: the Liturgy of the Word, the Adoration of the Cross, and Holy Communion. Within the Liturgy of the Word, there includes the Solemn Intercessions, which consists of ten specific intentions. They are 1. For Holy Church; 2. For the Pope; 3. For all orders and degrees of the faithful; 4. For catechumens; 5. For the unity of Christians; 6. For the Jewish people; 7. For those who do not believe in Christ; 8. For those who do not believe in God; 9. For those in public office; and 10. For those in tribulation. [MC14]

For my purposes here, I center on the sixth prayer offered on Good Friday for the Jewish people. It begins:

Let us pray also for the Jewish people, to whom the Lord our God spoke first, that he may grant them to advance in love of his name and in faithfulness to his covenant.

After a prayerful silence, the Prayer continues:

Almighty ever-living God, who bestowed your promises on Abraham and his descendants, graciously hear the prayers of your Church, that the people you first made your own may attain the fullness of redemption. Through Christ our Lord. Amen.

CHAPTER 5

In the second year of seminary at Pope St. John XXIII National Seminary, there was a required course each Tuesday, entitled, Pastoral Clinical Education, which included courses in the morning and then visits to an assigned hospital or nursing home facility in or around Boston. Each Tuesday I arrived at my assigned nursing home, and each day I passed a Jewish man in a wheelchair. Although I said hello, he never once spoke to me. Even though we wouldn't be ordained for three or four more years, the seminary required that we "look the part" by wearing the collar.

"Listen Israel: Yahweh our God is the one Yahweh. You shall love Yahweh your God with all your heart, with all your soul, with all your strength. Let these words I urge on you today be written on your heart. You shall repeat them to your children and say them over to them whether at rest in your house or walking abroad, at your lying down or at your rising: you shall fasten them on your hand as a sign and on your forehead as a circlet; you shall write them on the doorposts of your house and on your gates."[MC16]

Before the next visit the following week, I went to the seminary library and did some research. I wrote the first six Hebrew words of the First Passage of the Shema (Shema Yisrael, Adonai eloheinu, Adonai echad). After a slight pause, I would recite the words of Deuteronomy

6: 5-9, which stresses the commandment to love the Lord your God with all of your heart, soul, and might. The change in Mr. Silberberg* was instantaneous. Tears flowed from his eyes. I stopped and prayed the above prayer with Steve Silberberg*. I almost couldn't go on, but I did and finished the prayer. Every single Tuesday thereafter, when I visited that nursing facility until the end of the second spring semester, I stopped and prayed with Mr. Silberberg (this was not his real name, but for the sake of my memory, I'll call him this). [MC17] Lessons were learned for me well into the future through my experience with him. A smile, having an interest in him, and a reading from Deuteronomy were the keys that God opened up for both of us[MC18].

I have long since forgotten the name of the man in the nursing facility, but with his permission, I have borrowed the name of my close friend, Doctor Steve Silberberg, who was my eye doctor in Matawan until I retired on July 1, 2018.

CHAPTER 6

Near the cross of Jesus stood His mother and His mother's sister, Mary the wife of Clopas, and Mary of Magdala. Seeing His mother and the disciple He loved standing near her, Jesus said to His mother, "Woman, this is your son." Then to the disciple He said, "This is your Mother." And from that moment, the disciple made a place for her in his home (John 25-27).

I entered Pope St. John XXIII National Seminary in the fall of 1986 and completed the requisite four years of seminary in May of 1990. During those four years, many different courses were taught to help prepare seminarians for the many situations that a priest might experience. But some occurrences cannot be foreseen.

My first assignment after my diaconate ordination in 1990 was at St. John's Church in Lakehurst, N.J. My first priestly assignment was Our Lady of Sorrows Church in Mercerville, N.J. Future assignments would be Our Lady of Perpetual Help in Maple Shade, N.J., while also being named the Chaplain of Holy Cross High School, St. Anne's in Keansburg, N.J., and lastly, to Jesus the Lord Church in Keyport, N.J. for the next sixteen years. I retired from the active priesthood on July 1, 2018, and relocated to Port St. Joe, Florida. It happened that the two churches in Keyport, St. Joseph's and Jesus the Lord, merged to become Our Lady of Fatima on that very same day. My parish in Port

St. Joe is St. Joseph's. I'm unsure of its significance, but I am intrigued that technically all the parishes I served relate to the Crucifixion scene shown above.

My first parish, Our Lady of Sorrows, certainly taught me the sorrows that Our Lady [MC19] experienced and the universal need that *every* human person shares in. When Jesus speaks to His mother and to the disciple, His words were addressed to *everyone,* and that includes Edith Frank, Margot Frank, Anne Frank, and you and I. We may listen to Handel's Messiah or meditate on the sorrows that Mary experienced, but our lives should never be the same.

Joyful it was, but conditions were tough when Mary gave birth to Jesus. Fleeing to Egypt to escape Herod's pursuit and watching her Son despised and rejected, seeing Him stand trial and scourged at the pillar, and knowing His brow is pierced with thorns is impossible for us to comprehend. She heard His cry for thirst and watched His pierced hands and feet grow numb and livid. As we imagine this scene, we must be thankful for the disciple standing with her on that first Good Friday.

It is also here that we see Christ setting an example for children to honor their parents, and Mary is part of this experience. It clearly embodies love, affection, gratitude, and respect-and this is not just for young people. It follows us all of our lives. Christ's submission to His parents is not by accident.

Perhaps the years of obedience to His mother had ended, but not of honor. Jesus looks after her present necessities and future needs, but these qualities are equally part of Mary's concerns toward each and every person. I do believe that Mary and her Son were present for Edith Frank's, Margot Frank's, and Anne Frank's final moments. Their lived lives confirm my belief.

CHAPTER 7

Then

The number twelve in the Hebrew Scriptures is used in several ways, and perhaps most significantly, in its description of the twelve tribes of Israel in the Book of Genesis. It states that Jacob had twelve sons which later formed the twelve tribes of Israel: Reuben, Simeon, Levi, Judah, Zebulun, Issachar, Dan, Gad, Asher, Naphtali, Joseph, and Benjamin. The Bible confirms twelve sons of the patriarch Israel who each became the father of a tribe of the ancient nation of Israel.

In the New Testament, the twelve apostles are Andrew, the brother of Simon, Simon (or Peter), James, the son of Zebedee, John, the son of Zebedee, Philip, Matthew (or Levi), Nathanael (or Bartholomew), Thomas Didymus, James the Younger, Thaddeus (or Jude), Simon the Zealot, Judas Iscariot, and Matthias, the replacement for Judas Iscariot.

In watching the History Channel, the earth is depicted as having twelve dodecahedrons that connect the planet by electrical impulses, which Plato mentions in his writings. As this work centers on Anne Frank, I will show twelve biographies of saints that the Roman Catholic Church has declared beatified or canonized. The first saint that I begin with is the Blessed Mother of God, who is impossible to totally describe knowing that her life is celebrated in countless geographic areas, myriad cultural reasons by the veneration of specific icons, and the spectrum of so many human needs in so many situations. [MC20] I have chosen twelve titles for the Blessed Virgin Mary. Some are devotional, some are cultural, some are geographic, some are intercessory, some are dogmatic and doctrinal, and some are apparitional.

I have chosen Mother of God, Blessed Virgin Mary, Spouse of the Holy Spirit, Our Lady of Sorrows, Our Lady of Perpetual Help, Lady of the Immaculate Conception, Mary Help of Christians, Our Lady of Assumption, Our Lady Star of the Sea, Nuestra Senora de Guadalupe, Mary Queen of Heaven, and Theotokos (God-bearer).

In the Friday of the Passion of the Lord (Good Friday), the Church does not celebrate any sacraments at all, except for Penance and the Anointing of the Sick. The celebration of the Lord's Passion consists of three parts, namely: the Liturgy of the Word, the Adoration of the Cross, and Holy Communion. The Solemn Intercessions conclude the Liturgy of the Word with ten intercessions: For Holy Church; For the Pope; For all orders and degrees of the faithful; For catechumens; For the unity of Christians; For the Jewish people; For those who do not believe in Christ; For those who do not believe in God; For those in public office; and For those in tribulation.

I have shown below the Sixth Intercession of "For the Jewish people:"

> *Let us pray also for the Jewish people, to whom the Lord our God spoke first, that he may grant them to advance in love of his name and in faithfulness to his covenant. Almighty ever-living God, who bestowed your promises on Abraham and his descendants, graciously hear the prayers of your Church, that the people you first made your own may attain the fullness of redemption. Through Christ our Lord. Amen*[MC21].

CHAPTER 8

The Blessed Virgin Mary (1)

Mary, the mother of Jesus Christ, was born in Jerusalem around 20 B.C.E. As a young girl, she was betrothed to Joseph, a carpenter from Nazareth. Before they were married, the angel Gabriel appeared to Mary, telling her that God chose her to be the mother of the Messiah.

Some months after their betrothal, Joseph and Mary journeyed to Bethlehem for the census. Lodgings were crowded and the night was very cold. Knocking on many doors, they were always turned away. Finally, one kind innkeeper offered shelter in a stable. It was there that Mary gave birth to Jesus. King Herod heard of this and ordered that all male children under the age of two be put to death. An angel appeared to Joseph, prompting him to flee to Egypt for safety.

After Herod's death, the family returned to Nazareth. Every year, Jesus' parents went to Jerusalem for the feast of the Passover. When He was twelve years old, they went up to the feast as usual. However, Jesus soon became separated from His parents. Three days after, they found Him in the Temple, listening to the doctors and asking them questions. His mother said to Jesus: "My Child, why have you done this to us?"

To which He responded, "Why were you looking for Me? Did you not know that I must be busy with My Father's affairs?" (Luke 2:49). Mary knew that Gabriel's message was true.

Mary watched over her Son but watched others as well. At the wedding feast at Cana, Mary asked Jesus' help. At the crucifixion, Mary never left Jesus' side. When Jesus ascended into Heaven, Mary prayed with the disciples and was the first to see the descent of the Holy Spirit. We revere Mary as a gentle woman who bore great adversity with grace and strength.

As we celebrate Mary, the Mother of God, and as we reflect on all who lost their lives during the Holocaust, I believe that Blessed Mary, the Mother of God, was present with Edith and her children and with all who lost their lives with the atrocities of the Nazis in the Second World War.

Mary's Feast Day is celebrated by the Roman Catholic Church throughout the year, including January 1, March 25, August 15, September 8, and December 8. Mary is the patroness of motherhood.

Remember, O most gracious Virgin Mary, that never was it known that anyone who fled to thy protection, implored thy help or sought thy intercession, was left unaided. Inspired with this confidence, I fly unto thee, O Virgin of virgins, my Mother, to thee do I come, before thee I stand, sinful and sorrowful, O Mother of the Word, despise not my petitions, but in thy clemency hear and answer me. Amen

CHAPTER 9

St. Joseph- (2)
Then

The husband of Mary and the earthly father of Jesus, Joseph, was born in Judea or Galilee in the first century B.C.E. The Bible informs that the carpenter was a righteous man. When he learned his betrothed Mary was with child, he sought to end the engagement quietly, not wishing to expose Mary to public shame. That was his intention until an angel appeared to him in a dream, saying to him: "Joseph, son of David, do not be afraid to take Mary your wife into your home. For it is through the Holy Spirit that this Child has been conceived in her." And so, Joseph married Mary in obedience to God's will. Several months later, Joseph and Mary had to journey to Bethlehem to register for the Roman census.

With Mary nearing birth, this family was desperate to find a room in the crowded city. A goodly innkeeper offered them to use a stable nearby and Mary soon delivered a son. Soon, an angel in a dream warned Joseph to leave Bethlehem because King Herod threatened to murder all Jewish males under two years of age, seeking to kill the Savior before adulthood. Joseph took his family to Egypt until an angel gave him the all clear to return to Nazareth.

Very little is recorded of Joseph's influence on Jesus. Tradition certainly fills in some aspects of his role in Jesus' life, and the gospels tell us that Joseph and Mary brought Jesus to the Temple in Jerusalem each Passover and that he taught Jesus his carpenter trade.

Joseph is venerated as the guardian of the Universal Church, of carpenters, and of others, as well as the patron of a happy death since tradition says that Jesus and Mary were with him when he died. His feast day is celebrated March 19 and May 1.

> *Remember, O most chaste spouse of the Virgin Mary, that never was it known that anyone who implored your help and sought your intercession were left unaided. Full of confidence in your power I fly unto you and beg your protection. Despise not, O Guardian of the Redeemer, my humble supplication, but in your bounty, hear and answer me. Amen*

CHAPTER 10

Then
St. Anne de Beaupre- (3)

The mother of the Virgin Mary and grandmother of Jesus Christ, Anne, lived during the first century B.C.E., and it is believed she lived in Galilee and was of the tribe of Judah. Tradition holds that when she married Joachim, she promised to devote her first child to the service of God. She remained barren for many years. It would seem that Joachim, her husband, was disappointed and humiliated and, accompanied by servants, entered the desert to pray for months.

At last, an angel appeared to Anne, telling her that God had heard her prayers and that she would bear a child unlike any in the world. As she waited for her husband at the Golden Gate in Jerusalem, she was afraid with the angel's message. But when Joachim appeared, he seemed to know the good news of the forthcoming child, as the angel appeared to him as well.

As the angel had prophesied, Anne bore a daughter and named her Mary. Anne and Joachim soon moved to Jerusalem and at the age of three, dedicated Mary to the service of the Temple. Tradition holds that Mary walked up the Temple steps alone, without fear. With her act of dedication, Mary kept the promise Anne made when she married Joachim.

St. Anne and St. Joachim's feast day is celebrated on July 26, and she is honored as patroness of childbirth, homemakers, Canada and others. Frequently, she is depicted in art reading scriptures to Mary or teaching Mary to read.

> *Lord God Almighty, who hast given offspring to every creature, beasts wild and tame, to serpents, and birds, and fishes, and they all rejoice over their young ones, Thou hast shut out me alone from the gift of benignity. For Thou, O God, knowest my heart, that from the beginning of my married life I have vowed that, if Thou, O God, shouldst give me a son or daughter, I would offer them to Thee in Thy holy Temple. Amen.*[MC23]

"I can't imagine how anyone can say: I'm weak', and then remain so. After all, if you know it, why not fight against it, and why not try to train your character?"[MC24]- 4

CHAPTER 11

Then

St. Peter- The Rock- (4)

There is little known about the early life of Simon except that he was a Galilean fisherman and was probably born in the village of Bethsaida or Capernaum. When Christ was beginning His ministry, He was walking along the Sea of Galilee when He called out to Simon and his brother Andrew, "Come, and I will make you fishers of men" (Mt. 4:9).

Over the next three years Simon, called Peter, witnessed many miracles, including Jesus' curing his own mother-in-law of a fever. But Peter also failed to have faith, even bitterly at times. When Jesus approached the boat, walking on water, He beckoned Peter to come to Him, which he did, but then fear overtook him and he began to sink. As so often happened to Peter, he wanted to believe, but fear overtook him.

Fast forward to Gethsemane. Christ asked His disciples to stay awake while He prayed, but Peter fell asleep like the rest of the disciples. That same night, as Jesus had prophesied, Peter denied three times that he knew the Lord. Upon realizing that He had denied Him three times, he was overcome with remorse. He wept bitterly and vowed to change.

After Christ's Resurrection, He appeared to Peter and gave Him the awesome responsibility of continuing the Lord's work on earth. Peter embraced this challenge, knowing he would never be alone. His preaching began in Asia Minor in Antioch and continued ultimately to Rome, where he frequently had conflicts with the authorities. He became the first Pontiff and was martyred during the reign of Nero. Peter also laid the foundation for the Popes of the next two millennia, right up to the present day.

St. Peter's feast day is celebrated on June 29.

> *Gracious Father, by whose hand thy servant Simon Peter was most wonderfully delivered out of prison and impending death: Grant us, in all the changes and chances of mortal life, to dread nothing but the loss of Thee, and to cast all our care upon thee, who cares for us. When disasters lie ahead, help us to avoid them if we may, and to endure them if we must, knowing that we walk with Him, who endured all for us. Lord, we pray this to your Son, Jesus Christ, who now liveth and reigneth with Thee and the Holy Spirit, one God, for ever and ever. Amen.*

CHAPTER 12

Then

St. Martha- (5)

St. Martha was born around the time of Jesus' birth. She was the sister of Mary and Lazarus, whom Jesus raised from the dead. The Bible tells us that Jesus had a particularly close relationship with the three siblings, Martha, Mary and Lazarus, and loved them. Jesus had visited them at their home in Bethany, a small village two miles from Jerusalem.

Whenever Jesus came to visit, it was Martha who prepared the food and waited on everyone. Instead of helping Martha, Mary sat with Jesus and listened to Him. On one occasion, Martha even spoke to Jesus about this, hoping He would tell Mary to help her. But Jesus said nothing to Mary. Even though Martha remained focused on the household duties, she loved Jesus and truly believed He was the Son of God.

Four days after Lazarus died, Jesus came to Bethany to revive him. As Martha met Jesus, He told her He was "the Resurrection and the life." He reassured Martha and added, "whoever believes in Me will never die." When Jesus asked her if she believed this, Martha emphatically replied, "Yes, Lord, I have come to believe that you are the Messiah, the Son of God, the One who is coming into the world" (John 11: 25, 27).

According to western legends, after Jesus died, Martha went with her sister and brother to the south of France where they converted many to Christianity. It is also believed that Martha died in France. Her remains are said to have been found and enshrined there in the twelfth century.

St. Martha's feast day is celebrated on July 29. She is the patroness of homemakers, cooks, and others.

> *Martha, help me in the practical matters of life: home, work, family and friends. These are also things that make life worth living. Show me how to find comfort in committing myself to them and doing my best. Inspire me also to fine spiritual meaning within my own family, caring for and being with the ones whose identity is so intimately interwoven with my own.[MC26]*

CHAPTER 13

Then

St. Perpetua and St. Felicity- (6)

Perhaps the most moving of martyrdoms is St. Perpetua, a young mother who converted to Christianity in 203 A.D. At the beginning of the third century, it was most difficult to be a Christian. She was arrested and put in prison, which was dark, crowded, and unbearably hot. Being transferred to a slightly better place, her mother brought her infant son to visit. Perpetua was able to nurse him, but her father was very angry. He pleaded with her to renounce her faith so she could be freed. But Perpetua refused, "telling him that she trusted that her life lay in the power of God." [MC28] Finally, he took her son and refused to give him back.

At the time of Perpetua's arrest, a young slave named Felicity, who was eight months pregnant, was also arrested. To show her faith, Felicity desired to be tortured with others and worried that she'd be given more mercy because of her condition. Two days before her execution, she gave birth to a girl. Details of their respective imprisonments are preserved because Perpetua kept a journal. This was the first known written document by a woman in Christian history.

Indeed, her journal *The Passion of Saints Perpetua and Felicity* was so revered in the fourth century in North Africa that St. Augustine warned people not to treat it like the Bible. The morning Perpetua was forced to participate in the games at the Colosseum in Rome, she was composed and radiant, Felicity at her side. Perpetua refused to wear the traditional pagan costume, telling them she'd rather die than worship their gods. The crowd roared and the Christians were attacked-the men by a boar, a bear, and a leopard, and the women were attacked by a rabid cow. Both were badly wounded and were put to death by a soldier's sword. Perpetua's last words were to her brother: "Stand fast in the faith and love one another."

Perpetua and Felicity's feast day is March 7, and they are both the patroness of martyrs.

> *O God, the King of Saints, who didst strengthen thy servants Perpetua and Felicity and their companions to make a good confession, staunchly resisting for the cause of Christ, the claims of human affection, and encouraging one another in their time of trial. Grant that we who cherish their blessed memory may share their pure and steadfast faith, and win with them the palm of victory. Through the same Jesus Christ, our Lord, who liveth and reigneth with Thee and the Holy Spirit, one God, for ever and ever. Amen.*[MC29]

CHAPTER 14

St. Lucy (7)
Then

Throughout the ages, Lucy is one of the most venerated of all virgin martyrs in the Catholic Church. She is one of a very small list of saints included in the Roman canon, but there is no historical account ever put into writing. Her story is found as a legend recorded in the *Acts of Lucy*. It includes a description of how she was born to wealthy parents and also how her father died while she was still an infant. Lucy's mother, Eutychia, raised her by herself and had arranged that her daughter be married to a pagan nobleman.

Lucy took a vow of virginity at a young age, but her mother's efforts to have her daughter married were thwarted. In the ensuing days, Eutychia was stricken with an illness that lasted for four years. As she [MC31] prayed at St. Agatha's tomb, God cured her from her illness, and she gave thanks to God, which prompted Lucy to break her engagement and allowed her to distribute her wealth among the poor.

During Emperor Diocletian's persecution of Christians, Lucy was arrested and condemned to work as a prostitute in a brothel. After torturing Lucy and attempting to burn her, she still survived. Evidently, her eyes were gouged out, but they were miraculously restored. Finally, it is estimated that she died around the year of 304 A.C.E. from her wounds.

There are innumerable mentions of Lucy by early Christian writers. Many churches had been dedicated to her memory, most notably in Italy and the United Kingdom. St. Lucy is believed to be buried in a church in Venice, Italy.

St. Lucy's feast day is celebrated on December 13. She is the patroness of Syracuse, Sicily, the blind, authors, and others.

> *Lord, give us courage through the prayers of St. Lucy. As we celebrate her entrance into eternal glory, we ask to share her happiness in the life to come. We ask this through our Lord, Jesus Christ, your Son, who lives and reigns with you and the Holy Spirit, one God, for ever and ever. Amen.* [MC32]

CHAPTER 15

St. Leonard of Noblac (8)

Although details are lost to legend, Leonard was born a pagan in the 6th century and was a wealthy noble. It's said that he was offered a bishopric by his godfather, King Clovis I of France. It has also been said that he refused the offering, preferring to withdraw from society and to deepen his commitment to God.

One afternoon, King Clovis I and his wife joined a hunting party, entering a forest near Limoges where Leonard lived as a hermit. The Frankish people were a West Germanic tribe who worshipped pagan gods introduced by pagans. Word reached him that the queen went into labor and many prayers were offered. After much help, she gave birth to a healthy child. King Clovis I granted Leonard as much land as he could transverse in a single night. [MC34] Acquiring this land, Clovis founded a religious community and later built an abbey called Noblac. Many travelled to Noblac, particularly after word began to spread of many miracles occurring.

The compassionate Noblac preached to prisoners. Legend says that once Leonard deemed a captive as repentant, King Clovis I would agree to release them. Leonard became associated with prisoners of war. In the twelfth century, a French nobleman who had been imprisoned during the Crusades came to Noblac after his release. He paid tribute to Leonard by leaving silver chains like the ones he had worn in prison.

Leonard of Noblac's feast day is celebrated on November 6. He is the patron of women in childbirth, prisoners, and prisoners of war.

Leonard, humble servant of God, you opened your heart to everyone knowing that God's grace touches even the worst sinners once they acknowledge His love. By your example and the teachings of our Lord Jesus Christ, help me to show that some compassion, and help others grant me forgiveness when I wrong them. Amen.[MC35]

CHAPTER 16

Blessed Kateri Tekakwitha (9)
Then

The daughter of a pagan Mohawk chief and a devout Christian, Kateri Tekakwitha, lost her parents and a brother to smallpox when she was about four years old. This epidemic also left her partially blind and disfigured. At some point, Kateri went to live with an uncle. She vowed to never marry, for which she was shunned and mocked by her relatives.

Sometime around the age of twenty, Kateri met Jacques de Lamberville, a Jesuit missionary. This relationship profoundly affected her, and on Easter Sunday in 1676, she was baptized. As a newly converted Christian, she continued to be ridiculed and abused by many who were suspicious of this unfamiliar faith. She was frequently beaten and denied food because she refused to work on Sundays.

With Fr. Jacques' help, she escaped by walking across 200 miles of wilderness to reach the Christian American village of Sault Sainte Louis near Montreal, arriving in October of 1667. Kateri made her First Holy Communion on Christmas Day.

For the next three years, Kateri lived a prayer-filled life. As one missionary friend remembered her, she attended Mass twice each day and fasted two days each week. He also described her as having an insatiable thirst for spiritual knowledge and a soul disposed for perfection.

Kateri died peacefully around the age of twenty-four. Jesuit missionaries have attested to many miracles taking place around her grave. In 1980, Kateri Tekakwitha was beatified by (Saint) Pope John Paul II, the first Native American proposed for canonization.

Blessed Kateri Tekakwitha's feast day is April 17, and she is the patroness of ecologists, environmentalists, people in exile, and others.

O Jesus, who gave Kateri to the Native Americans as an example of purity, teach all to love purity, and to console your Immaculate Mother Mary through the Lily, Kateri Tekakwitha, and your Holy Cross.[MC37]

CHAPTER 17

St. Maximillian Kolbe (10)

Maximillian Kolbe was named Raimund when he was born in 1894. Having come from a very religious family, he had a vision that foretold his life when he was but ten years old. The Virgin Mother appeared to him and offered him two garlands, one representing virtue and the other representing martyrdom. Raimund declared he wanted both.

He joined the Franciscans in 1910 and chose the name Maximillian. He traveled to Rome to further his studies, and it was there that he deepened his love for Mary. In 1917, Maximillian and six other monks founded the Militia Immaculata, an organization dedicated to spreading Catholicism in Mary's name and whose members became the Knights of Immaculata.

When he returned to Poland in 1922, Maximillian published a magazine that promoted traditional values. Five years later, he founded the town of Niepokalanow, which translated to the "City of Mary the Immaculate." This town became the base for a media empire, which came to include a daily newspaper and a radio station. In 1931 he traveled to Japan and founded another city dedicated to Mary.

When Germany invaded Poland, the Nazis targeted not only Jews but also Catholic leaders and other groups. For several months, Maximillian was arrested and placed in detention camps, and although released for a brief period, he was arrested again in 1941 and sent to Auschwitz. He offered his life in place of another prisoner, and after being starved for two weeks, he was killed by lethal injection on August 14, 1941.

Maximillian Kolbe's feast day is August 14, and he is the founder of Militia Immaculata and the patron of twentieth century prisoners and others.

O Immaculata, Queen of Heaven and Earth, refuge of sinners and our most loving Mother, God has willed to entrust the entire order of mercy to you. I, repentant sinner, cast myself at your feet, humbly imploring you to take me all that I am and have, wholly to yourself as your possession and property. Please make of me, of all my powers of soul and body, of my whole life, death and eternity, whatever most pleases you. Amen.[MC39]

CHAPTER 18

St Theresa Benedicta of the Cross (11)

Edith Stein was born on October 12, 1891, in Breslau, Germany, which today would be Wroclaw, Germany. The Steins were Orthodox Jews, but Edith renounced her faith as a teenager and declared herself to be an atheist. She was a brilliant student and became one of the first German women allowed to enter a University. She first studied with Edmund Husseri, a world-famous philosopher and became his assistant.

Edith seemed destined for a distinguished academic career until 1921 when she happened upon the autobiography of St. Teresa of Avila, the foundress of the Reformed Carmelite Order. Having become familiar with St. Teresa's works, Edith was baptized into the Catholic faith and stopped working with Husseri and began teaching at a Catholic school.

In 1932, Edith accepted a lecturing assignment at a German University, but the following year, she lost her position because of anti-Semitic laws promoted by Adolf Hitler. She entered the Carmelite convent at Cologne and took the name Teresa Benedicta of the Cross. Teresa continued publishing her intellectual books and writing several other books. As 1939 began to dawn, growing dangers arose in Germany as anti-Semitism continued to rise.

Teresa feared reprisals for protecting Jews, so she transferred to a Carmelite house in the Netherlands. The Nazis began invading her new country and began to arrest all Dutch Catholics of Jewish descent. Teresa was sent to Auschwitz in 1942 where she was put to death in a gas chamber. Survivors of this camp praised her compassion for others who were facing death.

St. Teresa Benedicta of the Cross' feast day is August 9. She is the patroness of Europe, martyrs, and others.

> *O My God, fill my soul with holy joy, courage and strength to serve You. Enkindle Your love in me and then walk with me along the next stretch of road before me. I do not see very far ahead, but when I have arrived where the horizon now closes down, a new prospect will open before me, and I shall meet it with peace.*

CHAPTER 19

Saint Damian of Molokai, SS, CC (12)

Saint Damian of Molokai was born Josef de Veuster, a Catholic priest from Belgium and a member of the Congregation of the Sacred Hearts of Jesus and Mary, a religious institute. Damien's ministry began in 1873 and lasted until his death in 1869 in the kingdom of Hawaii. He lived and worked with people with Leprosy (Hansen's disease) and lived in a government-mandated quarantine in a settlement on Kalaupapa Peninsula of Molokai.

Damien taught the Catholic faith to the people of Hawaii and cared for the patients himself, dressing residents' ulcers, helping build reservoirs, making coffins, digging graves, and constructing roads, hospitals, and churches. He prayed daily before a picture of St. Francis Xavier, the Patron of Missionaries. Damien took the place of his brother, Father Pamphile, and travelled to Molokai.

When Father Damien arrived at the isolated settlement at Kalaupapa, where there were 600 lepers, he was presented by Bishop Louis Maigret. Upon arriving, Damien spoke to his assembled lepers, saying, "as one who will be a father to you, and who loves you so much that he does not hesitate to become one of you; to live and die with you." It is interesting to note that Alexandria Ocasio Cortez took some of her constituents on a tour of the Statuary Hall in the U.S. Capitol and pointed out the State of Hawaii's statue of St. Damien of Molokai and described him as an obvious example of a rich, white millionaire who lorded over the poor people of Hawaii. Obviously, she had no clue who he was.

Father Damien of Molokai's Feast Day is celebrated on May 10, although in Hawaii, it is celebrated on the day of his death, April 15. St. Damien of Molokai is the patron saint of the Diocese of Honolulu and of Hawaii and is the patron for leprosy and for outcasts.

St. Damien, happy and generous missionary, who loved the Gospel more than your own life, teach us to live our lives with joy like yours and to help the outcasts of our world. Help us to celebrate and contemplate the Eucharist as the source of our own commitment. Help us to love to the very end, and in the strength of the Spirit, to persevere in compassion for the poor and forgotten so that we might be good disciples of Jesus and Mary. Amen.

CHAPTER 20

Then and Now

I was assigned to Jesus the Lord parish on July 1, 2002, initially as administrator, and on January 3, 2004, I was installed as pastor of Jesus the Lord Church. During those seventeen [MC41] Christmases, I fulfilled a dream that I had had since I was a child. During each of those Christmases, I sang my favorite Christmas hymn, "In the Bleak Midwinter." In later years, I added one hymn, and near the end, two more (one in Spanish). But the last hymn directly before the final blessing was always "In the Bleak Midwinter."

Christina Georgina Rosetti wrote *A Christmas Carol* for the January 1872 issue of *Scribner's Monthly* and was first collected in book form in *Goblin Market* in 1875. The poem that Christina Rosetti composed was first to set to music, with the setting by Gustav Holst, some twelve years after her death in 1894. Since my arrival at Jesus the Lord parish in 2002, I have always maintained that the words created by Christina Rosetti in her poem, and the subsequent melody composed by Gustav Holst, captures the truth and beauty of that one holy night that all Christians revere as the most holy-when Jesus was born of the Virgin Mary as our Lord and Savior.

In the Bleak Midwinter

In the bleak midwinter, frosty wind made moan,
Earth stood hard as iron, water like a stone;
Snow had fallen, snow on snow, snow on snow,
In the bleak midwinter, long ago.

Our God, Heaven cannot hold Him, nor earth sustain;
Heaven and earth shall flee away when He comes to reign.
In the bleak winter a stable place sufficed,
the Lord God Almighty, Jesus Christ.

Enough for Him, whom cherubim, worship night and day,
A breastful of milk, and a mangerful of hay;
Enough for Him, whom angels fall before,
The ox and ass and camel adore.

Angels and archangels may have gathered there,
Cherubim and seraphim thronged the air;
But His mother only, in her maiden bliss,
Worshipped the beloved with a kiss.

What can I give Him, poor as I am?
If I were a shepherd, I would bring a lamb;
If I were a Wise Man, I would do my part;
Yet what I can I give Him, give my heart.

In her own diary words, Anne Frank was well aware of the Christmas story. Within it, she is seeking a trial lesson in "Elementary Latin." Her father asked Mr. Kleiman for a children's Bible so she could finally learn something about the New Testament. "Are you planning to give Anne a Bible for Hanukkah?" Margot asked, somewhat perturbed.

"Yes ... Well, maybe St. Nicholas Day would be a better occasion," her father replied. "Jesus and Hanukkah don't exactly go together."

Anne's last diary entry was on August 1, 1944. Some five months earlier, she confided: "'My dearest Kitty, the best remedy for those who are frightened, lonely or unhappy is to go outside, somewhere they can be alone, alone with the sky, nature and God. For then and only then can you feel everything as it should be and that God wants people to be happy amid nature's beauty and simplicity. As long as this exists, and that should be forever, I know that there will be solace for every sorrow, whatever the circumstances. I firmly believe that nature can bring comfort to all who suffer.'" -4

CHAPTER 21

Unbeknownst to Anne, her days continued to number. On March 31, 1944, she writes, "Hungary has been occupied by German troops. There are still a million Jews living there; they too are doomed."

I think it's odd that grown-ups quarrel so easily and so often and about such petty matters. Up to now I always thought bickering was just something children did and that they outgrew it.[MC42]- 4

CHAPTER 22

Now and Then: State of the World, 1941-1945

The morning of April 17, 1968, Mike Burke and I entered the annex, touring the place where the four Frank family members and five others hid out from the Nazis for more than two years. I didn't realize it at the time but experiencing that location, and subsequently meeting Anne Frank's father, would change my life significantly but not for quite a while. Anneliese Marie Frank was born on June 12, 1929, in Frankfurt, Germany. Today, Anne Frank would be ninety-two years old.

Otto Heinrich Frank was born on May 12, 1889. He was the second son of Michael Frank and Alice Betty Stern, who lived in Germany and were liberal Jews. Jewish traditions and holidays were valued, but they did not observe all religious laws. Otto's father owned a business bank in Frankfurt, and Otto, although briefly, studied art history in Heidelberg but soon after focused on traineeships at various banks, including Macy's in New York City.

Although initially it seemed as though the First World War had passed him by, Otto enlisted for Germany in 1915. He had been a part of a "Lichtmesstrupp," a unit that analyzed where enemy artillery fire came from. As the first World War was concluding, Otto was promoted to Lieutenant and was decorated. Upon his return from the war effort, he joined the family bank. Many years later, some eighteen months before his death in August 1980, he quoted to Basler Magazine, "After the experiences in Nagermany, we could live our own lives in the Netherlands. We were able to make a fresh start and feel fine."

Early in 1933, Otto and Edith Frank, perhaps glimpsing the handwriting on the wall, chose to leave Nazi Germany, particularly with business problems increasing but also due to the growing antisemitism of Adolf Hitler and that of his followers. Otto strived to build his company up while trying to provide for his family. Ongoing developments in Nazi Germany soon began to affect their lives in the Netherlands, and this was happening well before the annex hideout. The Franks sought the option of living in Great Britain but also desperately tried to immigrate to the United States with the help of a former student friend, desperate to escape the persecution of Jews. Unfortunately, all these options ended when the United States government entered the war on December 7, 1941, as all the borders were closed.

Feelings of freedom soon began to evaporate and then ended abruptly when the German army invaded the Netherlands in May of 1940. From that point onwards, the Netherlands was an occupied territory. New anti-Semitic measures were constantly being introduced, and it soon followed that Jews were not allowed to have their own companies. With the help of Otto's employees and Jan Gies, the husband of Miep Gies, he was able to keep his companies out of Nazi hands.

As the rest of 1941 continued and merged into 1942, the situation continued to worsen. Jewish men were arrested during raids and taken to the Mauthausen concentration camp. Many of those affected were friends and business associates of Otto and Edith.

As they officially began their stay on July 10, Edith and Margot were exhausted and had to sleep on bare mattresses. However, Otto and

Anne, the two cleaner-uppers began right away. Although, by Anne's own account, *"the place may be damp and lopsided,"* she observed that *"there's probably not a more comfortable place in all of Amsterdam, in all of Holland."*

The following day, Margot and her mother recovered somewhat, and they had their first meal, although Edith forgot about it, and soon it was scorched beyond saving. Despite Margot's constant coughing, they began to learn to live while they awaited the arrival of the Van Daans. On September 28, Anne first describes her ongoing fears as she wrote: *"Not being able to go outside upsets me more than I can say, and I'm terrified our hiding place will be discovered and that we'll be shot. That, of course, is a fairly dismal prospect."*

CHAPTER 23

Then and Now: State of the World

This chapter was written on October 10, 2021, one year and a day after I initially wrote Cardinal Dolan. The world is vastly different this October from last October. As I see it, the loss of freedom now rivals the loss of freedom that Anne Frank spoke of in *The Diary of Anne Frank.* Consider:

1. The freedom of travel.
2. The freedom of choice.
3. The freedom of speech.
4. The freedom of religion.
5. The freedom of life.
6. The freedom of conducting business.
7. The freedom of experiencing nature, God's green earth.
8. The freedom of self.
9. The freedom of healthy lives.
10. The freedom of safe borders.
11. The freedom of free will.
12. The freedom of education.

I remember when I attended Holy Cross School, a grammar school in Rumson, N.J. One of my teacher's emphasized that there was an eleventh commandment, namely, *Thou shalt not lie.* Sister Mary Dora was my teacher for fifth and seventh grade at Holy Cross School ('58 and '60). We would later be re-united at St. Ann's Church in Keansburg, N.J. when my third priestly assignment would occur and I became the Associate Pastor at St. Ann's Church in 1998. Her words, years later, made a lot of sense!

1. **The freedom of travel. Then:** Anne Frank, like all Jews in Amsterdam, were required to wear bright yellow buttons that immediately identified each person as one of Jewish descent. This meant that they could neither travel on the bus in Amsterdam nor could they ride their bicycles. Even walking on the street was very dangerous. Once they were forced to go into hiding, travelling anywhere was strictly in their dreams.

   Now: In 2021, in the United States of America, all citizens are allowed to travel only if they qualify under the requirements of the government, without being allowed to make their own decisions. This is required without benefit of natural immunity, of having already had COVID-19, or of following their physician's recommendations. It is far too frequently determined by government bureaucrats with no experience to make such decisions.

2. **The freedom of choice. Then:** The Jews automatically were denied the ability to choose for themselves to go where they wished, to purchase what they desired, or to visit family and friends. This God-given right was denied to them, and, of

course, Otto Frank was finally forced to enter the annex to try to escape their tormenters.

Now: When President Joe Biden was inaugurated on January 20, 2021, with a series of Executive Letters, the right to make certain choices, guaranteed by the Constitution of the United States of America, was denied to those same citizens of the U.S.A. It was mandated that vaccines must be given to each and every citizen without regard to individual choice, whether it concerned the advisement of medical professionals, doctor and patient privileges, their own physical health requirements, or their unique particular circumstances. It wasn't right then, and it isn't right now.

3. **The freedom of speech. Then:** The Jews, and other nationalities that soon followed, were not allowed to speak of conditions or even voice their opinions under fear of death and being hauled off to concentration camps. Putting up signs seeking help, employment, food-these all were forbidden to those living under the Nazi regime.

    Now: This past spring and summer of 2021 has seen the arrest of people exercising their freedom to speak about certain decisions that affected their lives, only to be punished for them. It seems as though the cognitively challenged President Biden is acting as a dictator and not as an elected President of the United States.

4. **The freedom of religion. Then:** In reading of the conditions and the causes of the Second World War, one of the most God-given rights denied by the rise of Nazism was the freedom to worship. This was forbidden to Jews and to other nationalities.

This began within Germany but quickly spread to other countries as citizens were seized and forced to relinquish their rights. This soon led to the mass execution of Jews, Catholics, and followers of other faiths through the many concentration camps set up in Germany and in other countries.

Now: As the spread of COVID-19 continued across the United States of America, the situation that developed found many cocktail lounges and bars open while houses of worship and synagogues remained closed. Other abhorrent developments were that many Catholic governors, congressmen, senators, and mayors of so-called blue states openly espoused abortions, which is the murder of innocents that first begun during the infancy of our Lord and Savior, Jesus Christ.

5. **The freedom of life. Then:** There was little or no effort to protect human life during the Nazi regime, as evidenced by the millions of Jews, Catholics, and Muslims who lost their lives on the streets of Amsterdam and in other cities, but quickly expanded to those millions who lost their lives in the concentration camps, either due to malnutrition-as was the case of Edith Frank, Margot Frank and Anne Frank-or outright slaughter in the ovens.

    Now: There are so many murders committed by so many in large cities, more frequently in so-called blue states. The murder of innocent life in the womb, or the unfavorable experiences in the womb are known and verified. Pregnant women are suffering right now, and this is one of the effects experienced by women living in the post-Trump period in our country.

6. **The freedom of conducting business. Then:** Any Jewish businessman living in Amsterdam was no longer allowed to conduct his business because of his Jewish heritage. As a case in point, Otto Frank was forced to have his business transferred to "officially" be filed under his gentile friends' names so he could continue to conduct his business in Amsterdam. He lived constantly in fear of being discovered and sent off to concentration camps.

Now: Under the current administration, requirements to "force" a small business with only a few employees to mandatorily receive the vaccine is driving so many companies out of business. These small businesses are being destroyed and with it, the lives of so many Americans. Some may have natural immunity, or they already may have had COVID-19 and survived. They may refuse, or they cannot take the vaccine due to their physician's doctor/patient confidentiality. But there are no such requirements for the thousands and thousands of illegal immigrants entering our country every day.

7. **The freedom of experiencing nature and God's green earth. Then:** Anne Frank frequently speaks of beauty, nature, sunshine, and the freedom to experience such things. She tells of the world being gradually turned into a wilderness and hears the approaching thunder which will destroy us too. She says she feels the sufferings of millions, and yet, if she looks up into the heavens, it will turn out all right. In the end, peace and tranquility will return again.

Now: Certainly COVID-19 has prevented the entire world from enjoying the beautiful nature that surrounds us. But restrictions have hampered our activities. They force masks on infants in day-care centers, forcibly reattaching them when they resist. Somehow, the love of God and the belief that God is with us through thick and thin seems to have vanished from too many people's lives.

8. **The freedom of self. Then:** Anne Frank was so affected by this. She admits to her "Dearest Kitty" that she has reached the point where she can hardly care whether she lives or dies. She acknowledges that the world will keep on turning without her and laments that she can't do anything to change events anyway. The irony of her feelings that she expressed in her Diary is that I began these efforts precisely because of her efforts that *did* change the world.

   Now: It has been reported that the number of suicides has increased in all age groups and among certain and different aspects of our society. Youth suicides, those serving in the military, suicides among the elderly, divorces increasing, marriages failing; people's hearts are lonely, and being together and helping each other out is a forgotten art. We must trust and help each other.

9. **The freedom of healthy lives. Then**: Times change. The nine individuals who sought to survive the conditions imposed upon them (by choice) and to know and enjoy the world they were born into were severely tested. I am sure each of them thought they would live to see a better day. But as time continued, it

must have sorely tested their spirits as each day lengthened into further gloom.

Now: With over 45 million suffering from COVID-19 and nearly three quarters of a million having passed away, the prospects for maintaining healthy lives is bleak to many. Mandatory vaccines are driving too many people into hopelessness and causing them to quit their jobs. The onslaught of winter for too many spells already tough lives getting tougher. [MC45] Something has to give.

10. **The freedom of safe borders. Then:** Anne Frank certainly overheard her father speaking about problems he had encountered while still living in Germany and when they emigrated to Amsterdam in Holland. As her family left their home in Amsterdam for the last time, wearing the many layers of clothing, Anne knew as a thirteen-year-old that they were no longer safe.

Now: For nearly a year, the borders of our country have no longer been safe as millions of people from around one hundred and fifty countries continue to pour over our southern border. They have penetrated our country, suffering with COVID-19, other sicknesses, and entering with deadly drugs. Something needs to be done, but there is no effort to solve these self-made problems.

11. **The freedom of free will. Then**: As Adolf Hitler and the Nazis continued to overtake countries throughout Europe, free will was removed from any individual who did not accept the Nazis' way. The Holocaust movement removed people, centering

primarily on Jews but others as well. At this time, the United States of America certainly believed and guaranteed each citizen the use of free will in making choices for their families, for each state in the union, and for all who entered our country. This has always been guaranteed in the Constitution of the United States of America, but this was not the situation with the Nazis.

Now: This is still guaranteed to every citizen of the United States. However, since January 20, 2021, this is no longer guaranteed. Ever since President Joe Biden proclaimed the words of the Oath of Office, this sadly, is no longer guaranteed. Indeed, no elected president or vice president since 2021 has yet to even remotely make any such attempts.

12. **The freedom of education. Then:** Even before the Frank family chose to enter the annex, going to school was fraught with many difficulties, especially trying to ride their bicycles or having to walk with obscene buttons that identified who they were. The Nazis were looking for any opportunity to thwart any Jews living in Amsterdam as their war efforts continued to escalate. In the annex, Margot and Anne continued to pursue their studies with by reading and writing. Initially, Anne Frank thought writing in a diary was for her own purposes, but later, after hearing radio broadcasts that encouraged those listening to write of their own experiences, she changed. Anne honestly believed they would be read, and she even returned to her previous entries to improve her writing for future readers.

Now: It seems ironic that Critical Race Theory (CRT) activists, actually by their own words, is replete with racism. It seems that the Universities in America have been leaning left for quite some time, and the inference also seems to imply that the curriculums across this country are steeped in socialism. The teaching of history today seems to be rewriting historical facts while, simultaneously, left-wing followers are tearing down statues with exclamation points and further destroying education in our country. Anne Frank looked forward to writing future history based on fact; ironically, she never could. But rewriting history this way must be stopped.

CHAPTER 24

[MC47]

1814[MC48]

Faith is the theological virtue by which we believe in God and believe all that He has said and revealed to us, and that the Holy Church proposes for our belief, because He is truth itself. By faith, "man freely commits his entire self to God." For this reason, the believer seeks to know and do God's will. "The righteous shall live by faith." Living faith "work[s] through charity."[MC49]

1815 The gift of faith remains in one who has not sinned against it. But "faith apart from works is dead:" when it is deprived of hope and love, faith does not fully unite the believer to Christ and does not make him [MC50] a living member of His Body.

> *"Where there's hope, there's life. It fills us with fresh courage*
> *and makes us strong again."*[MC51]

1817 Hope is the theological virtue by which we desire the kingdom of Heaven and eternal life as our happiness, placing our trust in Christ's promises and relying not on our own strength, but on the help of the grace of the Holy Spirit. "Let us hold fast the confession of our hope without wavering, for he who promised is faithful."

"The Holy Spirit...he poured out upon us richly through Jesus Christ our Savior, so that we might be justified by his grace and become heirs in hope of eternal life."[MC52]

1818 The virtue of hope responds to the aspiration of happiness which God has placed in the heart of every man; it takes up the hopes that inspire men's activities and purifies them so as to order them to the kingdom of Heaven. It keeps man from discouragement, it sustains him during times of abandonment, it opens up his heart in expectation of eternal beatitude. Buoyed up by hope, he is preserved from selfishness and led to the happiness that flows from charity.

1819 Christian hope takes up and fulfills the hope [MC53] of the chosen people, which has its origin and model in the *hope of Abraham,* who was blessed abundantly by the promises of God fulfilled in Isaac, and who was purified by the test of the sacrifice. "Hoping against hope, he believed, and thus became the father of many nations."

> *"I love you, with a love so great that it simply couldn't keep growing inside my heart, but had to leap out and reveal itself in all its magnitude."*[MC54]

1822 Charity us the theological virtue by which we love God above all things for His own sake, and our neighbor as ourselves for the love of God.

1823 Jesus makes charity the *new commandment.* By loving His own "to the end," He makes manifest the Father's love which He receives. By loving one another, the disciples imitate the love of Jesus which they themselves receive. Whence Jesus says: "As the Father has loved me, so have I loved you: abide in my love." And again: "This is my commandment, that you love one another as I have loved you."

1825 Christ died out of love for us while we were still "enemies," to make ourselves the neighbor of those farthest away, and to love children and the poor as Christ himself."[MC55]

1826 "If I ... have not charity," says the Apostle, "I am nothing." Whatever my privilege, service, or even virtue, "if I ... have not charity, I gain nothing." Charity is superior to all the virtues. It is the first of the theological virtues. "So faith, hope, charity abide, these three. *But the greatest of these is charity.*[MC56]

In my twenty-seven years of active ministry for the Diocese of Trenton, I probably celebrated hundreds of weddings. In all likelihood, the couple selected the reading quoted below probably roughly half of the time. It is from St. Paul's first letter to the Corinthians (1 Cor. 1-13) and from The Jerusalem Bible. It reads like this:

> *If I have the eloquence of men or of angels, but speak without love, I am simply a gong booming or a cymbal slashing. If I have the gift of prophecy, understanding all the mysteries there are, and knowing everything, and if have faith in all its fullness, to move mountains, but without love, them I am nothing at all. If I give away all that I possess, piece by piece, and if I even let them take my body to burn it, but am without love, it will do me no good whatever.*

> *Love is always kind and kind, it is never jealous; love is never boastful or conceited; it is never rude or selfish; it does not take offense, and is not resentful. Love takes no pleasure in other people's sins but delights in the truth; it is always ready to excuse, to trust, to hope, and to endure whatever comes.*

Love does not come to an end. But if there are gifts of prophecy, the time will come when they must fail; or the gift of languages, it will not continue for ever; and knowledge—for this, too, the time will come when it must fail. For our knowledge is imperfect and our prophesying is imperfect; but once perfection comes, all imperfect things will disappear. When I was a child, I used to talk like a child, and think like a child, and argue like a child, but now I am a man, all childish ways are put behind me. Now we are seeing a dim reflection in a mirror; but then we shall be seeing face to face. The knowledge that I have now is imperfect; but then I shall know as fully as I am known.

In short, there are three things that last: faith, hope and love; and the greatest of these is love.

CHAPTER 25

The words below were written by Woodie Guthrie in 1940 and set to music in 1945, one of the more famous American folk singers and the father of Arlo Guthrie. Woodie Guthrie was an inspiration to many during the depression years, perhaps most notably a young Bob Dylan, writing the majority of his poems and songs during this period. Although some might have described him as a communist, his main attribute was caring for the poor, especially during the Dust Bowl in the 1930's, particularly in Kansas and Oklahoma, the place of his birth. Woodie Guthrie served in the Merchant Marines, and shortly before his death on October 3, 1967, he asked Bob Dylan to write a song that themed the eternal search for hope. Bob Dylan responded with a 194-line poem called "Thoughts on Woodie Guthrie." Since I had begun my junior year at Loyola University of Rome in September of 1967, I decided it was an apt way to end this story devoted to Anne Frank by showing the words of "This Land is Your Land," written by Woodie Guthrie and released on January 1, 1940.

(Chorus)
This land is your land, and this land is my land
From the California, to the New York Island
From the Redwood Forest, to the Gulf Stream waters
This land was made for you and me.

As I went walking that ribbon of highway
I saw above me that endless skyway
I saw below me that golden valley
This land was made for you and me.

(Chorus)
I've roamed and rambled, and I've
followed my footsteps
All around me a voice was sounding
This land was made for you and me.

(Chorus)
When the sun comes shining as I was strolling
And the wheat fields waving and the
The dust clouds rolling
The fog was lifting a voice come chanting
This land was made for you and me.

(Chorus)
As I was a walkin'- I saw a sign there
And that sign said "No trespassin'"
But on the other side...it didn't say
Nothin!
Now that side was made for you and
Me!

(Chorus)
In the squares of the city- In the
Shadow of the steeple
Near the relief office- I see my people
And some are grumblin' and some are
Wonderin'
If this lands' still made for you and me.

(Chorus)
Nobody living can ever stop me
As I go walking that freedom highway;
Nobody living can ever make me turn back
This land was made for you and me.[iii]

I believe Anne Frank would've loved the lyrics of this song, and as it was first recorded in April of 1944, perhaps she heard it on the radio from London. Obviously, we'll never know, but I would like to think she did actually hear it. My very dear friends Bob and Alice who live in Fair Oaks, California told me of their neighbor, Bud (who I'd previously met, along with his late wife, Marie), who lived down the street from them and who tragically drowned in his pool. Sometime later, Bud's son, Travis, saw his father and mother in a dream together again in Heaven. That was enough of a sign for him. I've invested so much time mulling over Anne Frank, her sister, and her parents that I half expect that one of these days I will also dream of Anne Frank as a sign that she too is in Heaven.

The following weekend, Mike Burke and I traveled to Paris to meet up with my twelve-year-old sister, Janice, and although we visited the Eifel Tower, the best highlight of that day was when Mike and I rode bumper cars in Cleveland Square with Janice and one of her classmates.

I don't think Janice or I ever told our parents of spending April in Paris riding bumper cars! The last thing to end this story is to acknowledge that my entire year in Rome, I pursued and was in love with a girl at Loyola and even pursued her after Rome, but it never happened. I will only reveal her initials: *AMF!*

There are a number of people I would like to acknowledge and give thanks to: Timothy Michael Cardinal Dolan, Archbishop of New York. I am most grateful to Cardinal Dolan for his help and for steering me in the right direction.

Most Reverend David M. O'Connor, C.M., J.C.D., Bishop of Trenton. Thank you to Bishop O'Connell for his encouraging words as I continued to pursue this life-long project.

Most Reverend William A. Wack, CSC, Bishop of the Diocese of Pensacola-Tallahassee. Thanks to Bishop Wack for his diocesan leadership.

Reverend Michael Bellafiore, S.J., a formatter and teacher of systematic theology at Pope St. Pope John XXIII National Seminary in Weston, MA, ('1990) for his suggestions and insights into how to edify the final manuscript.

Brother William Martin, F.S.C., for his constant advice, suggestions, and recommendations during this entire project.

Steve Silberberg, M.D., O.D., for his permission to use his name for unnamed nursing home resident in Boston, MA, circa Fall, 1987/1988.

Patricia Pfleger of Jersey Printing for her timely and helpful suggestions concerning the world of printing in 2021.

Francesca of Huntington, WV and Lilly of Port St. Joe, FL, each for their respective interest in *The Diary of Anne Frank* and who I've selected as representatives of the millions of young people throughout the world who may be interested in reading Anne's diary or learning more about

Annelies Marie Frank's experiences at the annex in Amsterdam during World War II.

Flavia Medrut's *25 Anne Frank Quotes that Will Restore Your Hope*.

Hannah Tarwater, Advancement and Special Events Assistant at Rockhurst University, for her tireless help in trying to locate Michael Burke.

ENDNOTES

1. Much of the biographical material for saints from a 2 Volume set of <u>ORDINARY People EXTRAORDINARY Lives,</u> Inspirational Stories of the Saints;

2. Chapter 24, Sections 1814 and 1815, Faith; Sections 1817, 1818 and 1819, Hope; Sections 1823, 1825 and 1826, Charity, from the Catechism of the Catholic Church, 1994;

3. Woodie Guthrie, "This Land Is Your Land," 1951, *This Land Is Your Land*, phonograph record.

4. The various quotes used in this book are from Anne Frank's *<u>The Diary of a Young Girl</u>* or from *<u>The Diary of Anne Frank.</u>* [MC58]

---

[i] Much of the biographical material for saints from a 2 Volume set of ORDINARY People EXTRAORDINARY Lives, Inspirational Stories of the Saints;

[ii] Chapter 24, Sections 1814 and 1815, Faith; Sections 1817, 1818 and 1819, Hope; Sections 1823, 1825 and 1826, Charity, from the Catechism of the Catholic Church, 1994;

[iii] Woodie Guthrie, "This Land Is Your Land," 1951, This Land Is Your Land, phonograph record.